PORTLAND CASTLE

DORSET

'Right strong and magnificent castel'
(The Itinerary of John Leland, c.1535–43)

Portland Castle was built for Henry VIII between 1539 and 1540, to protect an important anchorage known as the 'Portland Roads'. Along with Sandsfoot Castle, opposite on the cliffs towards Weymouth, Portland was one of a chain of artillery forts built along the Channel coast to counter a feared invasion by France and Spain. Sandsfoot Castle suffered from cliff erosion soon after it was built and fell into ruin during the seventeenth century, but Portland Castle remained armed and garrisoned for nearly 250 years, and is still remarkably well preserved. The castle changed hands several times during the Civil War. It was maintained fitfully during the eighteenth and nineteenth centuries until the menace of invasion by Napoleon Buonaparte had passed. In the early nineteenth century, it was converted into a private house by the Manning family and some of the rooms were adapted for domestic use. However, with the development of the neighbouring Royal Navy base in the latter part of the nineteenth century, the castle returned to active service and remained in use until after the Second World War.

❖ CONTENTS ❖

Published by English Heritage, 23 Savile Row, London W1S 2ET
© English Heritage 2000. First published by English Heritage 2000.
Revised edition, 2002.
Photographs by English Heritage Photographic Unit and copyright
of English Heritage, unless otherwise stated.

Edited by Susannah Lawson
Designed by Pauline Hull
Printed in England by Westerham Press Ltd
C50 8/02 07559 ISBN 1 85074 725 3

TOUR OF THE CASTLE

❖

Portland Castle was built primarily for defence, and it was set close to the shore, giving it an excellent vantage point. The castle is shaped like a segment of a circle, with a two-storey circular tower or keep at its centre and rectangular wings radiating from either side. The main gun batteries were on two levels in the curved front towards the sea. A third tier of guns could be mounted on top of the central tower and its wings. This squat but powerful Tudor fort was equipped with the most up-to-date weapons, and could cross its fire with Sandsfoot Castle under two miles (about three kilometres) away on the other side of the bay. From an early date there was a moated and walled enclosure to the south of the castle. The castle has changed very little externally over the past four and a half centuries, apart from the enlargement of the original gun loops and windows in the early nineteenth century, when it was converted to a private house. When the castle was

registered as a historic monument in 1955, a decision was taken to show the interior as far as possible in its Tudor form. This meant stripping out the remaining nineteenth- and twentieth-century adaptations so that

Below: Aerial view of the castle, showing its unusual shape

Opposite: Fragments of painted lettering from Portland Castle

now there is little to see of the residence created by the Manning family or evidence of the castle's later wartime use.

After you have bought your ticket, you may wish to retrace your steps out of the captain's house and back through the gateway into the courtyard.

Courtyard

In the early eighteenth century, there was a house next to the outer gateway where the sutler lived; he sold provisions to the soldiers. Above the gateway is the coat of arms of Charles II, which was inserted in the original Tudor niche after the Civil War. It is made of lead and retains some of its original colouring.

Walk back through the gate towards the castle.

The building housing the ticket office, shop and tea room on your left was once the governor's brew house and stables, which were later enlarged to create the master gunner's house. This house was improved by the Mannings during the nineteenth century. In recent years it was used as the residence of the officer commanding HMS *Osprey*. Its interior has been greatly altered over the years, and it is now very difficult to get a picture of what it must once have looked like. It is now known as the captain's house.

Carry on down the path and cross over to the castle on the right.

The coat of arms of Charles II, set above the door of the outer gateway

The captain's house and the castle, seen from the gardens

Entrance

Immediately in front of the castle was once a moat. If you look up above the entrance, you will see a pair of long narrow slits which could have been for the chains used to raise a drawbridge. Below them is a Gothic porch, added in the nineteenth century, in front of the original entrance. The doorway inside is Tudor, although the door itself is Victorian. Just inside the door, the squared holes for the draw-bar securing the original door can be seen but they are now blocked with brick. The entrance passage is sharply angled as a security measure so that cannon shot could not be fired directly into the hall. The walls were plastered in the late eighteenth or early nineteenth centuries, but the plaster has been stripped back to the original masonry. In the passage on the left is a recess for the gun-loop which would once have protected the entrance. It was altered in Victorian times to make a window.

Step into the great hall.

Great Hall

This was the principal room on the ground floor of the castle, and would have been the main living room in Tudor times. On the far side of the room is a fireplace in front of which the life of the garrison would have centred. Although the central tower looks circular from the outside, the internal space is octagonal. The hall was very poorly lit by two cross-loops for hand-guns but these were cut back in Victorian times into larger windows. A prominent feature in the hall is the ornate central post. It was inserted to support the floor above and early plans show that there was another timber post in the same spot on the floor above supporting the gun platform.

Behind the central post is a timber and plaster partition which separates the hall from two small rooms. From the eighteenth century, they housed stores and military equipment. The three rectangular recesses in these rooms would have been used as store cupboards.

Fragments of stained glass from Portland Castle

A cross-loop in the gunners' quarters. The embrasure now houses a set of stocks

A display of seventeenth-century armour in the gunners' quarters

The gun room, where the main armament was positioned

On the right-hand side of the hall are two doorways. One leads to the kitchen in the south wing and the other to the stairs to the upper floor. On the left were the gunners' quarters or store in the north wing entered by a passage through the wall.

Go through the door to the left of the entrance, into the gunners' quarters.

Gunners' Quarters/Store

It is not entirely clear how this room was originally used. It might have served as quarters for the porter, or it might have been a store. After 1716, it was used as alternative barrack accommodation. Again, this is a very poorly lit room and the cross-loops were intended for close defence of the castle, not to light the room. The interior of the loops have slots for a bar across the centre and there are ledges in the frames at elbow height perhaps for manoeuvring hand-guns. In the far corner, and originally screened off from the main room, is a small angled room also with a cross-loop. It was probably a latrine.

In 1937, a cloakroom was installed off the entrance passage, complete with toilet and sink. The gunners' quarters now contain a display of seventeenth-century pikes, breastplates and helmets, which can be tried on. There are also reproductions of gunner's tools. There is a 'rammer' for forcing powder and shot down the barrel, a 'ladle' for inserting the gunpowder, a 'sponge' for washing out unburnt powder and a corkscrew-like 'worm' for removing traces of wadding after firing. There is also a small carronade type of gun in an embrasure.

Go up the stairs on the far side of the room.

Gun Room

This was the gun room, where the main armament was positioned. It is now open to the sky but it was originally roofed over to provide an additional upper gun platform. On the curving wall face of the keep there is a groove indicating a former roof line. The narrow windows of the keep were originally positioned above this line, but they were enlarged in the nineteenth century, cutting across the roof line. There is a groove in the wall of the keep just below, to carry the roof beams. At the far side of the room, there were originally some wooden stairs, shown on the plan of 1716 (on page 26), which gave access to the gun platform on the roof.

In the curving outer wall are five gun casemates. These are splayed to enable the guns to be moved, as they fired through the rectangular openings or ports. The gun-ports had iron hinges in the sills for wooden shutters. One shutter at the far end of the gun room has been restored. In the stone vault of the casemates are large vents to carry the smoke from the guns through 'chimneys' in the stone

Reconstruction drawing of the upper gun deck at Pendennis Castle by Ivan Lapper. The gun room at Portland was also originally roofed over

One of the guns has been set up with a reproduction set of gunners' rammer, worm and sponge and a restored shutter, to show how it would once have been used

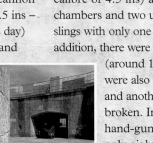

The remains of the brick hearth in the gun room

parapet above. A report dated 1779 listed five muzzle-loading guns mounted here firing a 12 lb shot. Today, there is an assortment of smooth-bore, muzzle-loading guns of eighteenth- and nineteenth-century date on reproduction carriages in the casemates. In the centre is a replica sixteenth-century saker, a gun whose muzzle was of around 3.5 inch calibre. There is also a garland of cannon shot and another reproduction set of gunners' rammer, worm and sponge.

The garrison would once have slept in the gun room. There are

traces in the pattern of stone paving and indications in early plans for four timber barrack rooms which were built against the keep. One of them served as a common room and had a fireplace, whose stone and brick hearth still remains. They were lit from above by roof lights. In the eighteenth century, the partitions were removed to allow greater space for handling the guns, and the gunners were moved to new quarters. There was a latrine for the gunners to the right of the door into the gun room, near the gunners' quarters.

❖ PORTLAND'S GUNS ❖

There is an inventory of the guns in all the royal castles, for the years 1547–8. At Portland, there was one brass demi-cannon (with a calibre of around 6.5 ins – one of the largest guns of its day) mounted with new wheels and equipped with a powder ladle and rammer. There were 30 iron shot and 80 lead shot for it along with serpentine powder. Two brass demi-culverin (of around 4.5 ins) also had new wheels, ladles and rammers. These were also well provided with ammunition. There were four breech-loading

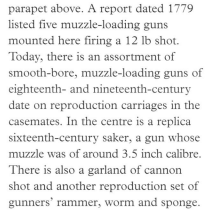

Cannon balls in the gun room

port-pieces (5.5 ins) each with two removable chambers. There was a Portuguese sling (a gun with a calibre of 4.5 ins) also with two chambers and two unspecified iron slings with only one chamber. In addition, there were three iron bases (around 1.2 ins) which were also breech-loaders and another which was broken. In terms of hand-guns there were only eight hagbushes but 23 bows of yew with 77 sheaves of arrows. Other infantry weapons were 29 fighting bills (an axe-like weapon) and 12 Moorish pikes.

Go down the steps through the opposite door.

Kitchen

This was the castle's kitchen, and the dresser, table and benches help give the impression of what it might once have looked like, although it would originally have been a smaller room than this. In the far right-hand corner is a large Tudor fireplace for cooking. The circular brick-lined oven on the left was probably inserted in the nineteenth century. In 1716, the kitchen was divided into three rooms – a pantry, cellar and kitchen. (Traces of partitions can be seen in the lines of black stones in the floor and in the sockets in the walls for a beam at floor level which divided the space into two.) The pantry was behind the kitchen, with a drain through the outer wall, and it was used for storing food. On the opposite side of the passage was a room formerly described as the cellar, used for storing wine or beer. From this room there might have been a serving hatch in the wall alongside the steps up to the gun room. There is a clear line of sockets in the east wall, behind the dresser, probably for racking for barrels. The windows in the kitchen would originally have been cross-loops, but they were enlarged in the nineteenth century. One Tudor cross-loop has been restored. An angled passage leads back to the great hall.

FOOD FOR THE GUNNERS

The food prepared in the sixteenth-century kitchen was likely to have been dominated by fish and the local mutton for which Portland was renowned. Archaeological excavations at Camber Castle, near Rye in Sussex, another of Henry VIII's coastal fortifications, have produced the bones of sheep, cattle, pigs, chickens, rabbits and several species of fish.

Otherwise bread and cheese would have been the gunners' staple diet.

The kitchen fireplace dates from Tudor times but the oven on the left was probably inserted in the nineteenth century

The castle's kitchen

The upper hall, which was originally the captain's hall. In Victorian times it was used as a dining-room

These stairs in the drawbridge chamber once led to the gun platforms on the roof over the keep

Right: This room was probably the captain's bedchamber in Tudor times, situated as it is next to the latrine

Return to the great hall down the passage.

A doorway immediately to the left opens on to a curving staircase leading to the captain or governor's lodgings on the floor above. The doorway is an original, unaltered Tudor doorway. The niches on the right of the stairs and at the top date from the nineteenth century, and might once have held lamps.

Go up the stairs and turn left when you reach the top.

Upper Hall

In Tudor times, this room would have been the captain's hall. The two small rooms on the right would have been servants' rooms. The layout of the room is similar to the great hall below. In Victorian times, this room was used as a dining-room, complete with a small butler's pantry in the window recess beside the stairs. The windows in the central recess, looking out over the courtyard, date from Victorian times. The niche might once have held a lamp.

Walk through the doorway opposite and turn left up the stairs just through the passage.

Drawbridge Chamber

The pair of long loops with circular openings at the top and bottom might have been for the chains of a drawbridge. This room would probably also have housed the winch

for raising and lowering the bridge. On the right are stairs leading to the original gun platforms on the roof over the keep and the wings. These steps have been cut off and by 1793 the platform had been replaced by a pitched roof. The wall on the opposite side has been altered in more recent times to provide access to the roof.

Go back down the steps and turn left into the next room.

Captain's Chamber

It has been suggested that this room might have been the quarters for the master gunner in Tudor times, but it is more likely to have been the captain's private chamber, situated as it is next to the only latrine on the first floor. The windows in the west wall have been altered since Tudor times, and the single window in the far wall was cut back to form a closet. It was here that a sixteenth-century inscription was found reading:

> God save King Henri the eight of that name and Prins Edward begottin of Quene Jane, mi

Ladi Mari that goodli Virgin, and the Ladi Elizabet so towardli, with the Kings honorable Cosels [Councillors].

In the early eighteenth century, this room was used as a dining-room, but by 1937 it had become a bedroom once again with a dressing room beyond. There was once a corridor here, and traces of the partition can be seen in the end walls beside the doorways. Above the corridor there is a ceiling dating from the eighteenth or nineteenth century and, partly hidden above it, is a projecting stone corbel which would have supported the original gun platform.

Go up the step at the far side of the room and down the step opposite.

Privy

This was the only latrine within the residential quarters. The discharge shaft can be seen from outside. In more recent times a flushing toilet was inserted into the head of the shaft.

Go up the steps to the upper gun platform. Take care as the walk-way can be slippery.

Upper Gun Platform

The sloping wall-walk is not original; there would once have been a roof over the gun room below. During the castle's active life, four guns could have been mounted on the roof behind the embrasures. These openings are wider than the gun-ports below, providing wider fields of fire, and they would have been suitable for

This was the only latrine within the residential quarters of the castle

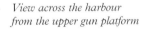

View across the harbour from the upper gun platform

This bell above the door to the kitchen dates from Victorian times, and was probably used for summoning servants

A distant view of the Portland Breakwater from the upper gun platform

guns on field carriages. Between the embrasures are the rectangular exits of the smoke vents from the lower casemates. These have now been covered over.

Looking across at the keep, you can see some original Tudor windows at first-floor level with their sills just above the former roof line. At the south end, above the windows, is a groove in the masonry indicating another, higher roof line. It might have covered some stairs which replaced, or were additional to, the now missing staircase in the northern corner. On the opposite wall, above the kitchen, is an external bell, perhaps for summoning servants, and probably dating from Victorian times.

Look up at the top floor of the keep.

From the wall-walk there is a good view of the curved parapet and embrasures of the former gun platform above the keep and its wings which provided a third tier of guns. On the parapet of the main block are curious clusters of stone balls. They are ornamental, and are meant to represent garlands of shot.

Portland Harbour

On a clear day, you can get an excellent view of the harbour from the upper gun platform. You can see the nineteenth-century breakwater, which created a harbour of refuge where whole fleets could shelter, as well as the sequence of fortifications that has protected Portland harbour for nearly 500 years. To the left are the ruins of Sandsfoot Castle, another Tudor castle on the other side of the bay. On the headland, jutting out in front of Weymouth, is Nothe Fort, built in the 1860s.

Ahead is the breakwater and its forts, partially hidden by the two concrete Phoenix Caissons, survivals of the D-Day preparations of 1944. Above, to the right, are the massive earthworks of the mid-nineteenth-century Verne Citadel with its great entrance arch. Looking down along the south side of the castle, is a small open, three-gun battery with a curved parapet and stone gun platforms behind. From here you can also appreciate the great mass of the Portland headland, the source of so much high quality building stone, and the quays and harbour of Castletown. In the other direction is Chesil Beach, its long causeway cut by a channel at Smallmouth which once separated the island of Portland from the mainland. For centuries, the island was connected only by ferry until the bridge was built in 1839.

Go through the door at the other end of the wall-walk.

Bedrooms

You are now in the east wing of the castle. These two rooms over the kitchen were once bedrooms. In Tudor times, they might have been the lieutenant's quarters. In the early eighteenth century, there was a corridor running between the two bedrooms, allowing access to the upper hall and beyond. The traces of this corridor can still be seen and one of the side walls remains

In Tudor times, this room might have been the lieutenant's quarters

between the two rooms. There is a fireplace in the larger of the two rooms on the left. By 1937, when the castle was used by the Royal Navy, it had become a sitting room. The smaller room on the right also has a fireplace, although it is simpler, and a large recess with the ends of six iron ties above it. The recess might once have housed a cupboard, but there is no obvious explanation for the iron ties.

When you have finished looking round these rooms, go back down the stairs to the great hall, where the tour began.

The Design of the Castle

You can get a good view of the castle from the sea shore, including the three tiers of gun embrasures, and the compact architectural and symmetrical composition, as well as the excellent masonry. Unlike in Henry VIII's other castles, little attention was given to close defence, apart from a moat which was filled in at an early date. The curious cross-loops on the ground floor intended for hand-guns are very archaic in appearance for Tudor times, and probably not very effective. (They are located mainly in the wings, with others on either side of the entrance into the central tower.) It is possible that they were, to some extent, merely symbolic of defence. The castle was later protected from the landward side by a moated enclosure.

To the rear is the walled courtyard, which was added to the original castle. It is now a garden,

but it was originally part of the defences. The northern side butts against the castle and partially masks the north-western cross-loops. An angled extension at this corner accommodated a platform for a single gun. The three-gun battery on the south is of the same date as the walled courtyard. The enclosure wall has a curved parapet like that of the castle. The captain's house is built over the parapet. At the time of the Civil War this moated courtyard would have provided a useful extra defence. The new governor's garden, designed by Christopher Bradley-Hole, lies beyond it to the south-east.

View of the castle from the sea

THE GARDENS
AT PORTLAND

History of the Grounds

Little is known about how the area immediately adjacent to the castle, enclosed by the outer wall, was used when the castle was first constructed. It might have been a gravelled yard area or it could have been grassed over but there is no evidence of it being used as a garden. The first buildings in this area were a sutler's house and the governor's brewhouse and stables, but these were remodelled into the master gunner's lodgings (or captain's house) in the early nineteenth century. It was probably at this time that the area now known as the captain's garden became a pleasure garden, rather than a functional yard. The quite separate governor's garden, beyond the castle wall, is shown distinctly as a garden as early as 1716 (see the plan on page 26) and appeared to be a walled area approximately half the size of the current garden. This was almost certainly used for growing vegetables and fruit. By 1835 this walled garden

had doubled in area to reach its present size and the pleasure gardens had been extended in front of the castle walls to what is now the road.

The governor's garden continued to be used by the Captain of the Royal Naval Station who lived in the captain's house until the station was closed in 1998; the garden subsequently fell into disuse. Even when the site was taken over by English Heritage in 1999, visitors were unable to use the governor's garden because of access and safety problems.

The rose beds at Portland in bloom, outside the entrance to the castle

RICHARD HADDLESEY

The new garden at the Medieval Bishops' Palace, Lincoln, designed by Mark Anthony Walker, is one of English Heritage's contemporary heritage gardens, like the one at Portland

The Contemporary Heritage Garden Scheme

The contemporary heritage garden scheme was initiated by English Heritage in April 1999, following the success of the Queen Mother's garden at Walmer Castle, designed by Penelope Hobhouse. Nine gardens are to be developed over five years with a budget of £1.5 million. Great care has been taken over the selection of suitable sites, as many of English Heritage's 400 historic properties are unsuitable for new gardens, either because of the need to protect buried archaeology, or because they are landscape or earthwork sites where new gardens would be inappropriate. Some of our major historic house sites already have nationally important historic gardens which are being restored, and so new garden overlays would be intrusive. Despite these restrictions, a number of properties have been identified that would benefit from a re-presentation of their landscape setting. As part of the brief, designers have been asked to respect the old as well as create the new, and to help encourage and develop an understanding of sustainable design in conservation work. It has been seen as a way of incorporating the work of the best contemporary garden and landscape designers within historic properties and improving the presentation of garden areas for visitors. So far English Heritage has opened contemporary heritage gardens at Osborne House on the Isle of Wight, Eltham Palace in London, Richmond Castle in Yorkshire and the Medieval Bishops' Palace in Lincoln.

The contemporary heritage garden scheme is continuing the tradition of gardening by providing a twenty-first-century layer of garden activity. By creating these new gardens we can show that it is possible to design something new without destroying the historic fabric of the site. Moreover, an attractive new garden can increase visitors and raise much-needed funds for conservation work. The scheme will also provide examples of the work of the best designers of today, to display to the visitors of the

Below: An artist's impression of the new governor's garden at Portland

...ygdaloides *(left) and the*
...ss Deschampsia caespitosa
...*en planted in the former moat*

Miscanthus *grasses (above) have been
planted in the lawn to provide movement*

future. There is obvious benefit in seeking the best designers, both newcomers and those already established, and in encouraging design competitions to further stimulate interest and debate.

Tour of the New Governor's Garden

The new governor's garden has been created by Chelsea gold medal winning garden designer Christopher Bradley-Hole. The garden aims to enhance the setting of the castle, and to provide a performance space, as well as a place for quiet contemplation. The design reflects the different aspects of the site. It is based on a circle of Portland stone with other elements relating to the ground plan of the existing buildings and to the north/south axis.

Visitors can enter the garden either directly from the outer courtyard, by walking across the end of the moat and through the gateway in the wall, or via the raised steel and timber bridge, which spans the moat and runs from the gun platform next to the castle directly into the garden.

Beneath the bridge is the former moat, which has been completely planted with bold swathes of the ornamental grass *Deschampsia caespitosa*, *Euphorbia amygdaloides* and the hardy white cranesbill *Geranium macrorrhizum* 'Album'. The bridge lands on an area of

Box has been planted beneath the pine trees

FLOWERPHOTOS © GILL ORSMAN AND CAROL SHARP

stone that intersects with a path of compacted gravel that encircles the central space. Visitors who enter the garden from the outer courtyard will be able to look along the moat to the steel and timber bridge, with the ornamental grasses below and the gun platform and sea beyond.

The focus of the garden is a large circular lawn that is surrounded by a circle of walls and seating to form an impressive amphitheatre. The seating is made of Portland stone that has been quarried locally, and laid as precise dry stone walls. The lawn is flat and cut into the sloping site,

providing a valuable performance space. The lawn is broken up by blocks of the large, ornamental *Miscanthus* grasses, which will grow to 1.8 metres high, and will provide constant movement in the garden as they sway and rustle in the wind and reflect the light. These blocks of grasses are on the points of the compass and reflect the maritime elements of the site.

To help enclose the space visually, and to protect it from the harsh elements, the existing screen of mature wind-sculpted sycamore trees has been enhanced by the planting of twelve new, semi-mature Corsican pine trees (*Pinus nigra* 'Laricio'). Beneath the trees is a grid of domed shrubs set in a swathe of grasses. These pines will eventually grow to 15 metres high and, like the existing mature trees, will develop a characteristic 'wind print' to show the direction of the prevailing winds.

A diagram showing the different planting in the garden at Portland

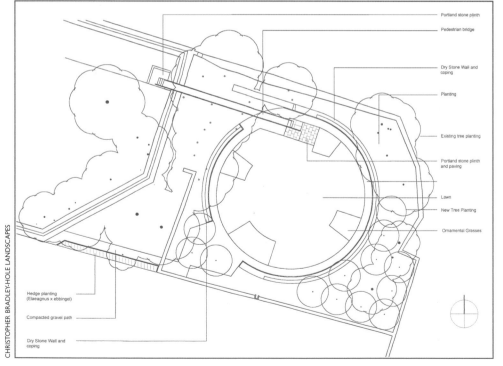

Portland stone plinth

Pedestrian bridge

Dry Stone Wall and coping

Planting

Existing tree planting

Portland stone plinth and paving

Lawn

New Tree Planting

Ornamental Grasses

Hedge planting (Elaeagnus x ebbingei)

Compacted gravel path

Dry Stone Wall and coping

CHRISTOPHER BRADLEY-HOLE LANDSCAPES

HISTORY OF
THE CASTLE

The Invasion Threat of 1539

Portland Castle was one of a chain of coastal artillery forts built by Henry VIII between 1539 and 1540. The project was known as 'the Device' and involved the fortification of parts of southern England from the Thames to Cornwall, paying particular attention to the protection of major anchorages. There was a real danger of invasion by the combined forces of France and Spain backed by the Pope. The divorce from Katherine of Aragon had led Henry VIII to declare himself Head of the Church in England, which, together with the seizure of the monasteries and their wealth, was an affront to these Catholic powers. For the first time in English history defensive measures were co-ordinated on a national scale. The fortification of the Dorset coast was recognised as an essential part of the anti-invasion measures. In April 1539, Lord Russell, one of Henry's leading advisors on

defence matters, surveyed the coast. The map he prepared included the locations of early-warning fire-beacons, as well as proposed sites for both Portland and Sandsfoot Castles.

A design for an artillery fort, 1539. The design of Portland Castle was a simplified version of this one

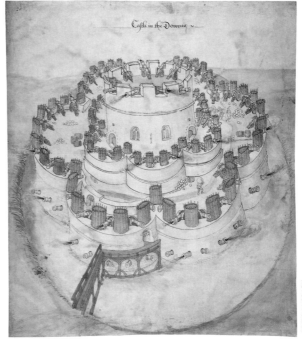

Portrait of Henry VIII, who instigated the construction of Portland Castle between 1539 and 1540

A detail from Lord Burleigh's map of 1539, showing beacons on Verne Hill and the proposed site of the castle

The 'Device' Forts

Portland is among the smallest of Henry's nine major castles. Like Deal and Walmer in Kent, and Hurst and Calshot Castles in Hampshire (all in the care of English Heritage), it is centrally planned with a round tower or keep as its nucleus, and it had three tiers of formidable firepower. Unusually, its outer gun platform does not go all the way round the keep, so it fails to have consistent all-round defence. Unlike Portland, Sandsfoot Castle was not segmental in shape, but had a rectangular residential block behind a polygonal gun platform. Although the two forts protected the Portland Roads, they could not cover Weymouth Bay to the north, and Weymouth was regarded as a weak spot. In 1545, Russell suggested additional gun batteries there and also asked for money to pay labourers at Portland, perhaps for the earthworks of the enclosed yard to the rear of the castle.

Building the Castle

For some of the 'Device' castles we have surviving building accounts which provide a glimpse of their construction. We are not so fortunate for Portland but we do know that work began on the 'Portland bulwark' in the summer of 1539 and was in progress in 1540, with the castle in a defensible state by December of that year. It cost just short of £4965,

Engraving of Sandsfoot Castle by the Buck Brothers, 1733

perhaps about £5,000,000 in modern terms. By comparison, Sandsfoot Castle cost £3887. The early garrison consisted of a captain (Thomas Mervin), four gunners and two others. The wages of a captain at the time varied between 12d and 24d a day; a porter was paid about 8d a day, and gunners 6d. Garrisons were often small, providing little more than care and maintenance for the guns, but they took in local forces in the event of an emergency. In around 1545, John Leweston was appointed lieutenant of the island and captain of the castle at 16d a day for life. This was the start of a long association between the captaincy of the castle and the administration of the island.

For the years 1547–8 there is a list of the guns and munitions in all the royal castles. These include a wide variety of muzzle- and breech-loading

RULES AND REGULATIONS

There were detailed rules and regulations laid down for all Henry VIII's forts. These concerned the number of days the captain, deputy and porters were allowed to be absent in a month without loss of pay. Two gunners and soldiers were to keep watch every night and if found sleeping or absent were to lose two day's wages for the first offence. The opening and shutting of the gates was regulated according to the season of the year, depending on daylight hours. No gunner was to shoot off ordnance or summon any ship without the command of the captain, and captains were not to extract any payment from ships in transit or when anchoring in the Roads. None of the garrison was to indulge in hunting and no one was to make an affray at the gates or on the walls on the pain of imprisonment. Everyone had to provide himself with appropriate weapons. Gunners therefore had to have a hand-gun or 'hagbush' of their own. Musters of the garrison and inventories of munitions were to be taken quarterly.

pieces with unfamiliar names. As part of the stores there were crowbars and sledges and gynne's with brass pulley blocks for mounting ordnance.

Neglect and Decay

After the early years of tension and enthusiasm, there was a familiar and continuing story of neglect and lack of maintenance. In 1574, a commission of inspection under Lord Howard of Bindon found Sandsfoot going to ruin, the walls cracked by frost and in danger of falling into the sea. At Portland 'bothe the plateformes...are in lyke dekeay and ruine as the other... and the leades of the same castell is also very muche in dekeaye never repaired or renewed synce the...house was first erected beinge 34 yeares past'. Nothing was done, and in 1583 another survey showed further deterioration in the fabric of both castles. Between 1584 and 1586, with the threat of invasion from Spain hanging over the country, £228 was

The Armada off Portland, 1588

spent at Portland in overhauling the castle. During the crisis of 1588, when the Armada was moving up the English Channel, the second clash between the two fleets occurred off Portland Bill. It was a moment of panic for the local population, who feared that the Spanish might put into the Roads. Fortunately, the Armada was defeated. Shortly after 1588, the captaincy came into the hands of Sir Walter Raleigh. Although he was an absentee, he did recognise the castle's potential and the need for effective armament. With the Spanish menace still present in 1596, the garrison is listed as a captain, two porters, six gunners and five soldiers.

In 1623 there was a thorough survey by Sir Richard Morryson. This provides the most detailed account of the castle and its physical state since its construction. There were 13 guns of various sizes (three culverins, nine demi-culverins and a saker). In addition, there were 20 muskets with another 34 classed as unserviceable. The garrison was made up of a captain, lieutenant, two porters (one for the inner entrance and another for the outer gate), master gunner and a number of other gunners. The lieutenant was asked to explain why a bronze cannon was missing and why ten men were found to be absent. The main defects to the fabric of the castle were caused by the sea. In addition, the roof of the keep had

deteriorated so badly it was recommended that, instead of having a flat lead roof, it should be replaced by a sloping tiled roof, especially since guns were no longer mounted on top of the keep. Half the lodgings for the gunners were decayed. The moat around the courtyard was overgrown and had to be dug deeper and wider and enclosed on the inner side with a stone wall. The moat had to be repaired with a bank acting as a sea wall. The castle and other fortifications along the south coast were surveyed at this time by Dutch engineers, who drew up a plan of the castle. By 1636, two more long-range guns had been added to the complement and the garrison was listed as a captain, a lieutenant and 11 soldiers and gunners.

View of the castle and the gun platform from the east

Soldiers of the New Model Army in a Civil War re-enactment at Kirby Hall. The island of Portland was a Royalist stronghold, and control of the castle passed between the Royalists and the Parliamentarians over the course of the Civil War

Civil War

The island of Portland was a Royalist stronghold. At the outbreak of the Civil War in 1642, forces loyal to Parliament took control of the island and the castle but in the following year the castle was taken by deception by a party of Royalists disguised as Parliamentary forces. In 1644, a Parliamentary campaign into the West Country led to a four-month siege before the castle was relieved by the Royalists. With the Navy loyal to Parliament, it was important that the anchorage was not controlled by Royalist Portland. With this in mind there was another unsuccessful attempt to take the castle by Parliamentary forces the next year. Finally, Colonel Thomas Gollop surrendered to Vice-Admiral William Batten in April 1646. As was customary with a negotiated surrender, the Royalist garrison was allowed the 'honours of war' and marched out with their personal weapons, colours displayed and drums beating. Only five of the garrison

actually set out for the Royalist headquarters at Oxford suggesting that the great majority were local men.

After the Civil War, the Commonwealth maintained the castle and in 1651, in addition to a gunner and gunner's mate and two quarter gunners, there were 100 soldiers of various ranks attached to it. In 1653 orders came for all military works in Portland to be destroyed except for the castle, in order to stop the Royalists rising again. The castle played a key role in protecting the anchorage in the First Anglo-Dutch War in 1653, when there was a three-day sea battle off Portland. The castle was used as a prison for prominent Royalists and the future Duke of Lauderdale, a Scottish Royalist, was confined there after the Battle of Worcester between 1655 and 1657.

With the Restoration of Charles II in 1660, the garrison was reduced to its previous manning level of captain, lieutenant and 11 soldiers and gunners. The royal coat of arms was erected over the gateway and in 1665 a warrant was issued for the castle's repair at the outset of the Second Dutch War. By 1679, there were 16 guns present, all requiring new carriages and platforms. The isolated garrison found various forms of additional employment. One of the soldiers, John Peters, acted as Portland's customs officer until, in 1681, he was found to be in league with local smugglers.

SMUGGLING

Smuggling was common among Portlanders. It flourished particularly during the eighteenth and early nineteenth centuries and often led to violence with the Revenue men. Portlanders used to go out to sea to meet French boats and transfer contraband. More people from Portland were committed for smuggling offences than from any other part of Dorset.

Smugglers Landing in a Storm, 1791, by Philip James de Loutherbourg

VICTORIA ART GALLERY, BATH/BRIDGEMAN ART LIBRARY

Protection against Privateers

By 1702, the castle was said to be in a very dangerous condition. In his survey of 1715, Colonel Lilly, a military engineer in the Office of Ordnance, described the platforms in both 'lower and upper keepes' as having to be replaced. Two years later the armament was reduced to seven guns. Sandsfoot Castle was by then in total ruin. In 1725, Portland's role was described as protecting trading vessels against privateers. Indeed, in 1704 its main function was said to be providing protection for the boats carrying stone for the building of St Paul's Cathedral in London.

The use of Portland stone for public buildings, especially in London, had steadily increased since the architect Inigo Jones had adopted this material early in the seventeenth century at the Banqueting House in Whitehall.

An engraving of the Banqueting House, Whitehall, designed by the architect Inigo Jones. He was one of the first to use Portland Stone for public buildings

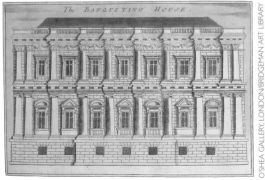

O'SHEA GALLERY, LONDON/BRIDGEMAN ART LIBRARY

Plan and views of Portland Castle in 1716

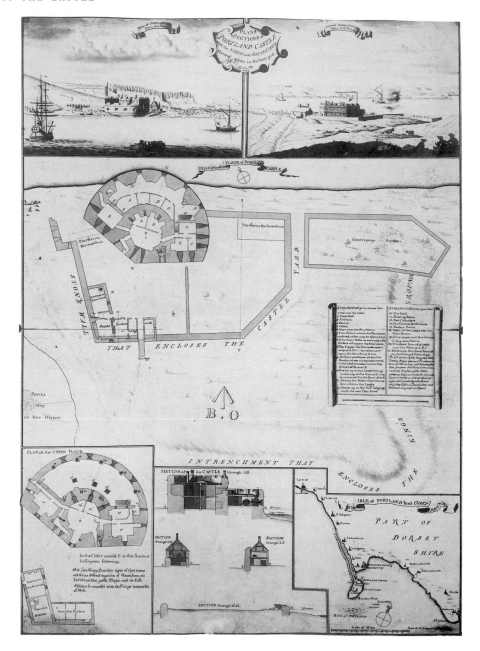

(Caption at right:)

View of Portland Castle by J. Upham, c.1802 (detail). This is one of a set of 18 views of the island made for the then governor, John Penn

The stone quarries came to provide the main source of employment for the islanders. The quays and jetties for the stone trade lay close to the castle which was their only immediate protection.

This muted state of affairs continued during the eighteenth century. A report of 1779 listed three guns on the external platform to the south of the castle and five guns in the casemates in the gun room. They were said to be in pretty good condition but needed painting. The garrison now consisted of a master gunner and two quarter gunners in what must have been a purely caretaking role. There had been no repairs to the castle for 30 years. The roof leaked and the timber in places was much decayed. There was, however, a small dry magazine and storeroom at the top of the castle. In the 1790s, during his visits to the fashionable seaside resort of Weymouth, George III came to Portland on several occasions and the guns of the castle were fired in salute.

With the threat of Napoleon's invasion in the early years of the nineteenth century, the armament in the castle was considerably increased. In 1805 there were six 24-pounders, six 12-pounders and two 9-pounder guns but this was the last time the castle was armed.

The Manning Episode

In 1816, with the war with France over and less need for coastal defences, the Commander-in-Chief, the Duke of York, with the agreement of the Master-General of the Ordnance, granted the castle to the Reverend John Manning, a prominent islander, for a 'marine residence'. It was then very dilapidated and a considerable sum was spent on renovating it, both

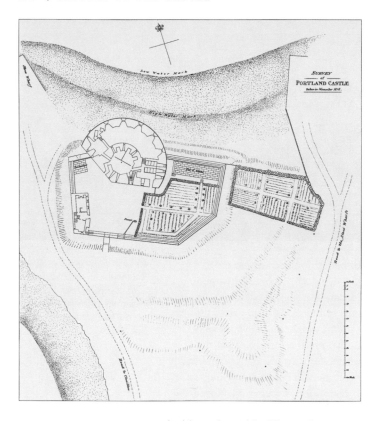

Plan of Portland Castle in 1816

inside and outside. These changes are to be seen today in the enlarged windows and battlemented walls round the gardens. John Manning died in 1826 and in 1834, his son, Captain Charles Manning, was granted the castle and made governor by the king following the death of another prominent local citizen and island governor, John Penn. Captain Manning lavished attention on the castle and installed a collection of fossils, weapons and examples of his skills as a wood-carver. He was the last

governor of the castle. His activities on behalf of the islanders as lieutenant of the island and resident magistrate, founder of the Mechanics Institute, chairman of the Portland Dispensary, President of the Literary Institute and builder of several public buildings, brought him great respect and affection.

The Breakwater and the mid-nineteenth-century Fortifications

The dangerous coastline and the continuing heavy losses of ships and lives had led a certain John Harvey in 1794 to propose the construction of a breakwater to give greater security to the Portland Roads, creating a safe harbour. Material to build the breakwater was readily available on the island; the huge quantities of capstone or quarry waste could be used. There was later an additional political reason for creating a harbour of refuge. France had begun the construction of a massive naval base at Cherbourg and it was thought that the building of a breakwater at Portland would give the British navy complete command of the English Channel. In 1844, in the year the breakwater in Plymouth Sound was completed, a plan to convert the Roads into a harbour of refuge was formed. Captain Manning was closely involved in the project. Work was begun in 1848 using convict labour for quarrying and transporting the stone required. The establishment of a prison on the island was primarily for this purpose. The breakwater was later extended across the harbour until it was completed by the end of the century.

The foundation stone of the breakwater was laid by Prince Albert on 26 July 1849 at the suggestion of Captain Manning. As lieutenant of the island, Manning met the Prince Consort on several occasions, during his many visits to Portland to see this feat of nineteenth-century civil engineering. The Victorian period was a time of great inventions, and Prince Albert took a particular interest in new developments. With the building of the breakwater came the provision of new defences, which protected the harbour, taking over the castle's defensive role. In 1852 there was a suggestion for a fortress on the Verne, 500 ft above sea level, overlooking the harbour and Weymouth Bay. A vast ditch was cut,

Engraving from the Illustrated London News, *1884, showing convicts at work in the quarries on Portland*

Engraving from the
Illustrated London News,
*1872, showing Prince
Albert fixing the last stone
of the Portland Breakwater*

*Opposite: Photograph of
bombs being dropped over
Portland in the Second
World War*

isolating a portion of the commanding heights, with the spoil going towards the construction of the breakwater. Behind the ditch a great rampart was constructed with capacious bomb-proof barracks below. The Verne became a citadel, a central point of defence, with detached gun batteries which would stop the enemy using the harbour. At the same time other defences were created on the breakwater itself: Breakwater Fort and Inner Pier Head Fort. On the Weymouth side of the harbour was Nothe Fort. Later, in 1893, came additional batteries (known as A, B and C Pierheads) to counter the threat of torpedo-boat attack at the time when the construction of the centre and north arms of the breakwater was sanctioned. Around 1900 came new breech-loading gun

batteries at Upton and Blacknor. Portland Castle was left unarmed but in the midst of an expanding system of modern fortifications.

Portland in Two World Wars

The castle subsequently returned to military and naval use. With the death of Captain Manning in 1869, the War Office took back the castle for use as an army residence and for a number of years it was the home of the adjutant of the Verne Citadel. With the increasing development of the harbour as a naval base, particularly during the First World War, Portland was a location for the manufacture and testing of torpedoes and then served as an anti-submarine base. In 1917, a Royal Naval Air station for seaplanes flying anti-submarine patrols was established on the mere beside the castle. The castle meanwhile was used as an ordnance store. Between the wars, Portland Harbour was the assembly point for the Atlantic and Home Fleets, and the castle returned to use as a residence. During the Second World War, Portland was the main anti-submarine base and HMS *Osprey* was the centre for underwater warfare and detection. With the war came air raids on the island and notably, in 1940, the sinking of the auxiliary anti-aircraft ship, HMS *Foylebank*, within the harbour (the Foylebank collection is now in the care of English Heritage). As the issue of national survival eventually turned towards the liberation of occupied Europe, Portland was used as a base for training in combined operations (land, sea and air forces) with landing craft in 1942. By 1943, landing craft hards, for beaching boats, were being constructed and preliminary training for the D-Day landings was carried out in the two bays on either side of Portland by both British and American forces. The two Phoenix Caissons, opposite the castle near Castletown Pier, were intended for the Mulberry Harbour off the Normandy coast. Throughout

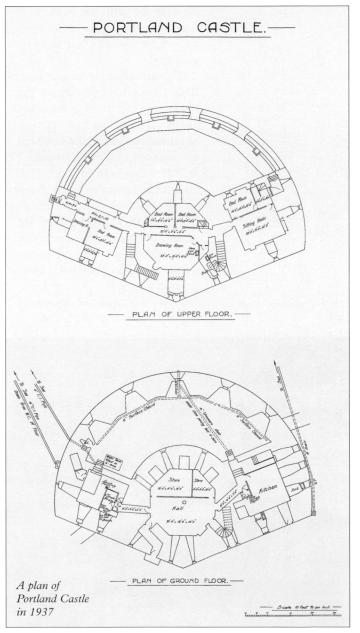

— PORTLAND CASTLE. —

— PLAN OF UPPER FLOOR. —

— PLAN OF GROUND FLOOR. —

A plan of Portland Castle in 1937

this time, the castle was in use as both living quarters and offices for both British and US military personnel.

The airfield and helicopter base of HMS *Osprey* developed greatly after 1945 but by the 1990s its importance had dwindled and the 150-year Royal Naval association with Portland has now come to a close. The castle opened to the public in 1955. The captain's house, however, continued to be the residence of the commanding officers of HMS *Osprey* but this, the gardens and the courtyard are, once again, part of the castle, allowing visitors to explore the whole castle complex for the first time, and to discover more about the castle's key role in the history of the island.

The gun platform from the east

Bibliography

E A Andrews and M L Pinsent, 'The coastal defences of Portland and Weymouth', *Fort*, 9, Supplement, 1981, pp.4–43

H M Colvin (ed.), *The History of the King's Works*, IV, 1485–1600, Part II (1982)

John Hutchins, *The History and Antiquities of Dorset*, 1863

Stuart Morris, *Portland: An Illustrated History*, 1996

The Royal Commission on the Historical Monuments of England, *An Inventory of the Historical Monuments in the County of Dorset*, Volume II, South-east Dorset, 1970

Andrew Saunders, *Channel Defences*, 1997

Victoria County History of Dorset, II, 1908

Genevieve Wheatley, *A Teacher's Handbook to Portland Castle*, 1994

Acknowledgements

English Heritage is grateful to Mr Stuart Morris for information on the recent history of the castle.